Published by
Lion Hudson Limited
Wilkinson House, Jordan Hill Business Park
Banbury Road, Oxford OX2 8DR, England
www.lionhudson.com

ISBN 9780745977935

First edition 2019

A catalogue record for this book is available from the British Library.

Printed and bound in China, September 2019, LH54

Albert
and the
Big Boat

A Noah's Ark Story

Written by Richard Littledale
Illustrated by Heather Heyworth

LION
CHILDREN'S

Albert was an elderly mouse. He wouldn't have liked you to say so, of course, but that is what he was. His fur was growing a little thin, and his coal-black eyes didn't twinkle as much as they used to. There was a kink in one of his whiskers, and the tip of his tail had a piece missing from the day when the cat nearly caught him.

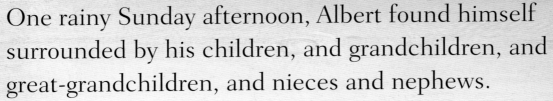

One rainy Sunday afternoon, Albert found himself surrounded by his children, and grandchildren, and great-grandchildren, and nieces and nephews.

"Tell us a story," they clamoured.

"A story?" said Albert.

"Yes," they all squeaked back. "Tell us the one about the boat, the great big boat."

"The one about the great big boat," Albert chuckled, and made himself comfortable on his best pile of shredded tissues.

When he could see that every eye was focused on him, every tail was tucked away neatly where it couldn't twitch, and every coal-black pair of eyes was on him, he began.

"It all happened a long time ago," he said. "Long before our grandfathers, or their grandfathers, or even their great-great-grandfathers walked the earth. Back then, the world was still quite new. Many animals had no name, many were hidden away in deep caves or high on mountains, and all should have been well."

"But it wasn't," squeaked Benjamin, the youngest mouse
in the room (who had heard the tale before).

"No," said Albert, "it wasn't. People were cruel and silly and selfish, and nothing was the way it ought to be. That's when God decided to start all over again. When the day came he would make it rain and rain and rain until everything was washed away for a clean new start."

"What about the boat?" whispered Abigail, a little white mouse with a teeny tiny voice.

"Ah yes – the boat," continued Albert. "God told his friend Noah to build a boat. It was to be the biggest boat that anyone had ever, ever seen. Its sides would be taller than the tallest tree, its deck would be wider than the widest river, and inside there would be lots and lots of room.

"For weeks on end there was hammering and banging and sawing and fixing as the boat took shape. Giraffes would crane their tall necks to look down inside. Spiders would weave webs up the scaffolding just so they could see what was going on. Birds would swoop overhead to look at the great boat, and even a cat managed to slip inside one day."

At the mention of a cat, the little mice booed and hissed loudly.

Albert waved a paw for them to be quiet. "When the day came," he continued, "it was time to board the great big boat. Every kind of animal, from wombats to worms and kangaroos to kookaburras, was to have a space on board."

"What about mice?" squeaked George, a little brown mouse at the back of the crowd.

"Oh yes," said Albert, "there were certainly mice. They raced up the gangplank, dodging between the elephant's feet, jumping over the cobra's back, scuttling across the lion's paws, and found a nice little corner all to themselves.

"And that is where they stayed for forty days and forty nights. The wind blew, the waves crashed, and that great big boat pitched up and down like a fairground ride – but it never, never broke.

"When the storm ended and the waters went down, God told Noah to open the door and let all the animals out. Up above them a rainbow stretched across the sky. God said, 'As long as you can see a rainbow when it rains, you know that there will never be a storm like this one ever again.'

"With that the animals all made their way to their nests and burrows and hidey-holes, wherever would suit them best… and they never travelled together on the big boat again."

All the little mice fell silent. It was quiet outside too, for the rain had stopped. At first one, then another, and another, and another turned to look out of the window high up above them. Stretched across the sky was a great big colourful rainbow.

They all scampered outside to look, leaving Albert to settle down for a nap on his best shredded-tissue seat.